Series / Number 04-026

Political Reasoning
in Adolescence:
Some Bridging Themes

RICHARD M. MERELMAN
University of Wisconsin

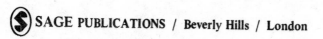 **SAGE PUBLICATIONS** / Beverly Hills / London

For information address:

SAGE PUBLICATIONS, INC.
275 South Beverly Drive
Beverly Hills, California 90212

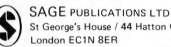

SAGE PUBLICATIONS LTD
St George's House / 44 Hatton Garden
London EC1N 8ER

International Standard Book Number 0-8039-0538-6

Library of Congress Catalog Card No. 74-27565

FIRST PRINTING

When citing a professional paper, please use the proper form. Remember to cite the
correct Sage Professional Paper series title and include the paper number. One of the
two following formats can be adapted (depending on the style manual used):

(1) NAGEL, S. S. (1973) "Comparing Elected and Appointed Judicial Systems."
Sage Professional Papers in American Politics, 1, 04-001. Beverly Hills, and London:
Sage Pubns.

OR

(2) Nagel, Stuart S. 1973. *Comparing Elected and Appointed Judicial Systems.* Sage
Professional Papers in American Politics, vol. 1, series no. 04-001. Beverly Hills and
London: Sage Publications.

CONTENTS

Political Reasoning
in Adolescence:
Some Bridging Themes

RICHARD M. MERELMAN
University of Wisconsin

I. INTRODUCTION

A description of some "bridging themes" in adolescent political thought is the major intent of this paper. The term "bridging themes" refers to several constellations of political thinking that result from the interaction of two main aspects of adolescent maturation: (1) cognitive development, and (2) personality development. Bridging themes occur because adolescent personality conflicts create individual variation in the normal development of political reasoning during adolescence.

I believe that the uncovering of bridging themes may aid us in unifying our theoretical approaches to political socialization. Heretofore a chief impediment to such unity has been our tendency to divide the study of maturing political identifications and affects from the study of maturing political cognitions and reasoning. This separation can be observed from the very outset of socialization research. Most of the important early work on political socialization concentrated almost entirely on identifications, preferences, affects, and attitudes (Greenstein, 1968: 551-555; Schonfeld, 1971: 544-578). In psychoanalytic summary, this research focused on the

AUTHOR'S NOTE: *This article is a revised version of a paper first presented at the 1973 Annual Meeting of the American Political Science Association, New Orleans, La. Support for the research from which this paper is drawn came from the National Institute of Mental Health under Grant No. 1 RO1 MH20627-01.*

origins and vicissitudes of political cathexes, especially those involving authority and partisanship. As Koeppen has pointed out, the early emphasis had a lasting effect. For most of its brief history political socialization research has retained its fascination with "feelings," broadly construed, rather than with ratiocination (Koeppen, 1970: 545-564). Little attention has therefore been paid to psychological models of reasoning; most efforts have relied, usually implicitly, on a Freudian model of development, in which emotive and motivational factors, not cognition or comprehension, played a key role.

Only in recent years has the development of political reasoning begun to emerge as a common topic of research in political socialization.[1] This emergence has been stimulated by our growing awareness of, respect for, and application of cognitive developmental theory in psychology.[2] Unfortunately, this new focus has suffered from the same errors as its Freudian predecessor. Where the latter largely excluded reasoning from its purview, the former has, for the most part, excluded motivation. In the process, the cognitive developmental approach to political socialization has generally ignored psychodynamic factors that might affect the formation of political reasoning.

Any reconciliation between or integration of these two approaches has also been hindered by their differing temporal foci. Socialization research directed towards understanding political affects and identifications has usually followed the Freudians by concentrating on the childhood years, while research aimed at political reasoning has followed the developmentalists by concentrating on late childhood and adolescence.[3] Rarely has a piece of socialization research attempted to encompass both childhood and adolescence, perhaps because of an implicit realization that different underlying theoretical models would render such a complete account of socialization very difficult indeed.[4]

Yet, because socialization is a single process that encompasses both reasoning and feelings, a reconciliation of these two approaches is not only possible, but highly desirable. Consider adolescence as a critical socialization period, for example. The developmental model of adolescence concentrates on the maturation of reasoning during this period, while the less well-known psychoanalytic approach to adolescence describes critical changes in adolescent emotional structure (Gallagher and Harris, 1958). But, of course, these processes do not operate in isolation from each other. In fact, they can be found commingled in any substantive area—such as politics—where learning takes place during adolescence. Therefore, we must utilize both the psychoanalytic and cognitive developmental models in order to understand adolescent political reasoning fully. The bridging themes I will describe are meant to illustrate this proposition.

Before turning to a discussion of these themes, however, it is necessary to describe in detail the two models of adolescent maturation whose joint influence we shall be depicting. Let us begin with the cognitive developmental approach. To the developmentalist, adolescence is a critical period because it brings about the transition from concrete to formal operational thought. Concrete thought is characterized by the child's inability to reason about problems beyond his immediate experience, by his lack of abstractive capacity, and by his inability to understand the functions of rules, hypotheses, or deductions. By contrast, formal reasoning moves the adolescent beyond the familiar and permits him to think abstractly, hypothetically, and deductively (Inhelder and Piaget, 1958). The formal reasoner is thus in a position to internalize general rules, to judge consistently, and to apply universal norms to individual cases.

The transition from concrete to formal reasoning is a complicated process that involves the mastery of many separate reasoning skills. For most middle class adolescents in the West, the transition occurs between the ages of eleven and thirteen, although some aspects of formal reasoning do not usually fully develop until late adolescence in most people, while a minority of people never truly become formal reasoners in any real sense.

Three particular aspects of this transition are of special interest to the student of political socialization:

(1) role-playing,

(2) moral reasoning, and

(3) abstractive capacity.

As to the first of these, developmentalists argue that the transition from concrete to formal reasoning occurs in part because of the child's newfound ability to take the role of others and to move away from a purely egocentric conception of society to a sociocentric conception (Flavell, 1968; Elkind, 1969: 497-507; Adelson and O'Neil, 1966: 295-306). As to the second, the developmentalists argue that the young child is dominated by an authoritarian conscience which binds him to a rigidly traditional, punitive view of morality (Piaget, 1965). Only when his newfound role-playing capacity permits him to take the role of others can he arrive at moral judgements that are not only comparatively benign but are also based on such general concepts as reciprocity or natural rights. Therefore, not until adolescence will most children have a fully-internalized conception of fairness or of the Kantian categorical imperative. Finally, the developmentalists claim that role-playing and moral maturity help to *decenter* reasoning from the self, thus making the adolescent capable of

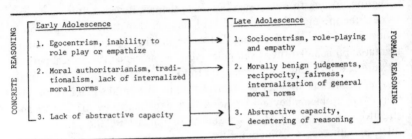

Figure 1: THREE ASPECTS OF THE COGNITIVE DEVELOPMENTAL SCHEME OF ADOLESCENCE

comprehending impersonal abstractions, such as those found in mathematics and logic (Witkin, et al., 1962).

Figure 1 sums up these three aspects of the cognitive developmental approach to adolescence. The relevance of these three types of cognitive development to political reasoning should be obvious. Role-playing bespeaks a capacity to appreciate the point of view of political opponents and to sympathize with their dilemmas, while sociocentrism implies an acceptance of the truly *collective* nature of political problems. Moral judgements play a part in many political decisions, not only among policy-makers but also among the general public, particularly when the latter find themselves evaluating the demands put forth by different groups in the pursuit of governmental benefits. In addition, of course, an appreciation of general moral rules underlies the notion of a legal system. Finally, abstraction provides a strong foundation for consistent ideological thinking about politics.

As I have suggested, the psychoanalytic approach to adolescent maturation concerns itself primarily with the vicissitudes of the adolescent's emotional life. To the psychoanalytic investigator what is critical about adolescence is the coming of puberty. In the West, at least, puberty is both a biological and psychological wrench to the young adolescent, so much so, in fact, that it ushers in a turbulent, three-phase developmental sequence highlighted by a resurgent Oedipal conflict, sex role differentiation, regression to narcissism, transient homosexual identifications, and spasmodic ego development (Blos, 1962). Most contemporary psychoanalytic theory agrees that adolescence is fraught with conflicts as severe as any experienced during the height of the earlier Oedipal phase. In Josselyn's summation, "Adolescence is probably psychologically the most complex maturational phase in the normal individual's development" (1971: 19-20).

A convenient way of conceptualizing the emotional upheavals of adolescence is to follow Havighurt by outlining the developmental "tasks" the normal adolescent undertakes.[5] Personality theorists have addressed themselves to three such tasks:

(1) sex role identification,

(2) impulse control, and

(3) adoption of a social identity either through rebellion against or conformity to parents and society.

Let us consider each task in turn.

Puberty forces the adolescent to come to terms with sexuality. This task requires management not only of highly charged biological drives, but also of the social roles constraining the expression of sexuality. After all, "masculinity" and "feminity" are, at least in part, the work of society. Not surprisingly, therefore, the normal adolescent must spend much of his time attempting to adapt himself comfortably to the biological and social demands that puberty has suddenly thrust upon him.

The young adolescent experiences the efflorescence of sexuality partly by resurrecting the earlier battles of the Oedipal and Electra complex (Blos, 1962). These complexes encompass two main drives: desires to possess the opposite sexed parent and to punish the same sex parent. Understandably, drives of this sort can be controlled only by the most strenuous exertions. American adolescents often channel these drives into calls for greater independence from parental controls, into highly competitive sexual or quasi-sexual activities, and into a renewed taste for violence and self-assertion expressed in sports or, occasionally, in delinquency. In sum, adolescence not only forces an accommodation to sex roles but also provides a stern test of impulse controls.

But above all, as Erik Erikson has pointed out (1968), adolescence is the time when society presents the individual with the problem of social identity. In part, this confrontation is a by-product of the other two tasks we have already described. Efforts at sexual accommodation and impulse control almost inevitably face the adolescent with a choice between two conflicting social identities: rebel or conformist. The adolescent may choose either to subjugate his impulse life and manage his sexuality so as to conform to society's expectations, or he may choose to express his impulses uninhibitedly and to defy social expectations. Usually, these two alternatives are first explored against the continual backdrop of parental authority. Propelled by pressures from their peers, most adolescents first stake out an identity vis-a-vis their homes and then move on to society as a whole. The key question is whether the adolescent will accept his parents and their values or whether he will rebel and try to establish a distinct identity of his own. Figure 2 sums up the psychoanalytic model of adolescence.

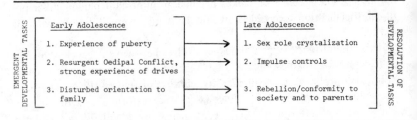

Figure 2: ASPECTS OF THE PSYCHOANALYTIC SCHEME OF ADOLESCENCE

As I have suggested, the importance of personality restructuring in adolescence appears to have escaped the cognitive developmental approach to political socialization. Most who have investigated the growth of political reasoning in adolescence have done so with scant regard for the emotional turbulence of adolescence itself. Consequently, we have implicitly assumed that individual emotive idiosyncracies and typical personality tasks have no lasting effects on political reasoning. We have been all too content to presume instead that eventually most adolescents somehow learn to apply "formal" reasoning to politics. Unfortunately, we have rarely tried to explain why the evidence on adult political reasoning does not support this presumption.[6]

There have been attempts to recognize the possible long-term effects of personality factors in adolescent development, but they have usually been half-hearted and ritualistic, more afterthought than theory. I have in mind here particularly Kohlberg's recent (1969: 397) flirtation with "role-taking opportunities" or Peel's vague allusion to research on the role of personality in adolescent reasoning (1971: 152). The modal position is more that of Adelson and Beall (1970: 495-504), who conclude rather smugly that age alone is a major determinant of adolescent political reasoning.

It is particularly critical that this gap in the developmental approach be filled immediately, lest it inhibit the capacity of the developmental model to take its newly recognized place in the study of political socialization. From its tentative introduction in the works of Dawson and Prewitt (1969: 51) and Hess and Torney (1967: 21-22), the developmental approach has become the centerpiece of full-scale theoretical exercises by Merelman (1969) and Best (1973: 48-70). The work of Adelson and his colleagues (1971: 183-201) as well as that by Haan, Smith, and Block (1968: 261-288), has provided important evidential support for the utility of the developmental approach. Finally, Harmon's recent work (1973) established a crucial empirical link between Kohlberg's theory of moral development and fundamental aspects of political judgement. The developmental approach now bids fair to become an important paradigm for political socialization research. It would be a pity were it flawed when it did so.

It is, therefore, time to build some bridges between the psychodynamic consideration of adolescence and the cognitive developmental approach to political socialization. Although the developmentalists themselves have been slow to undertake this task, two recent efforts are favorable harbingers. I am referring to the recent article by Kohlberg and Gilligan (1971) and to R. W. Connell's (1971) innovative book.

Kohlberg and Gilligan's major thesis is that, under the stress of contemporary social stress and consequent adolescent identity diffusion, the normal but temporary regression to childish hedonism among adolescents can rigidify, causing permanent damage to moral development. Kohlberg and Gilligan view such damage as particularly likely today, primarily because of countercultural influences that disturb normal development and alienate young people. Unfortunately, the authors' use of Erikson's identity crisis notion does little to clarify the actual psychological dynamics of developmental retardation, but at least Kohlberg has finally begun to focus upon the possibility of permanent alteration in such developmental "universals" as moral judgement.

Connell's book takes us one important step further. Connell describes several processes of emotional development in childhood that parallel and occasionally intersect the child's developing mental picture of politics. The most interesting example of this phenomenon is the "threat motif." According to Connell (1971: 202):

The idea of an external threat to the country . . . becomes charged at an early age with personal emotion, with fears of violent intrusion into the "nice" and "safe" places of the child's own life. We will not be far out if we trace the affect laden threat schemata of later childhood and adolescence to these roots. At later ages, naturally, as the children construct an image of the political order, the threat is placed more firmly in a political context.

What Connell here suggests is a link between the child's emotional vulnerability and the occasional absence of mature, flexible political reasoning in adolescence. There is, after all, good reason to believe that children who experience threats especially keenly will have difficulty acquiring the role-playing and empathic skills of formal political reasoning. Although Connell explains that the perception of external threat has deep roots in Australian history, he never intends to dispel the impression that personality differences among children will determine receptivity to the "threat motif." Indeed, he intends precisely the opposite.

Mode	Description	Measurement Techniques
Abstract Thought	Use of general, formal concepts in the characterization of a policy problem, as opposed to concrete language, examples, personal experiences, etc.	Based on responses to initial question asking how respondent would explain the problems of poverty or prison disorders to someone who knew nothing about these subjects.
Causal Thought	Ability to construct a coherent sequential explanation of a policy problem	Based on responses to question asking about the causes of poverty or prison disorders
Effect Thought	Ability to construct a coherent sequential explanation of the effects a policy problem has on society	Based on responses to question asking about the effects of poverty or prison reform
Moral Thought	The capacity to justify one's policy preferences by reference to universalistic norms of reciprocity or moral principles rather than by hedonistic calculation of external effects	Based on responses to question asking what should be done about poverty or prison difficulties
Social source Thinking	The ability to locate the source of a social problem in distinctly social institutions or collective actions, rather than in personal predilections or frailties	Based on responses to questions asking who or what was responsible for poverty and prison disorders
Definitional Sociocentrism	The willingness to allocate a collective entity, such as government, the right to define the extent of a social problem	Based on responses to a question asking how responsibility for defining the extent of poverty and prison problems should be assigned
Role Taking	The capacity to construct arguments contrary to one's own policy preference	Based on responses to question asking what arguments a person who disagreed with the respondent about poverty or prison reform would employ
Linkage Thought	The capacity to see the effects of a distant social problem on the circumstances of one's own life	Based on responses to questions asking whether the individual was aware of any effects that the existence of poverty or prison difficulties had on him or his family
Hypothetical Thought	The capacity to imagine the effects of removing a social problem. This ability involves reasoning about a contrary-to-fact situation, i.e. the world minus the problem at hand	Based on responses to questions asking the individual about how the United States would be different if there were no more poverty and no more problems associated with prisons, such as prison riots, etc.

Figure 3: THE COMPONENTS OF POLICY THINKING*

These two recent studies have provided me with guidelines for the effort represented in this paper. My main concern will be to link together the three forms of maturation described by developmentalists and summarized in Figure 1 to the three adolescent motivational tasks outlined by psychoanalysis and summarized in Figure 2. I shall try to show how these processes intersect and jointly influence the course of political socialization. To do so I have extracted three bridging themes from a particular body of interview material which now requires discussion.

In the spring of 1972, I conducted 236 open-ended interviews about poverty and prison reform with 118 seventh and twelfth graders in Madison, Wisconsin. These interviews form the heart of an investigation into the growth of adolescent "policy-thinking." Policy-thinking refers to nine cognitive modes by which political problems may be apprehended and evaluated. Each mode was defined by reference to cognitive developmental theory, and the scheme as a whole was viewed as a political analogue to the reasoning skills discussed by developmentalists (Merelman, 1969; 750; 1971: 1033; 1973: 161; Merelman and McCabe, 1974). Figure 3 describes the nine forms of policy-reasoning in detail.

Despite the well-known difficulties encountered in coding open-ended interviews, final results of the analysis generally conformed to the cognitive developmental model of socialization. Policy-reasoning, both methodologically and theoretically, fits developmental assumptions.[7] Nevertheless, careful reading of each interview transcript revealed that the typical adolescent personality problems outline in Figure 2 had had an impact on policy-reasoning. Though unexpected, these impacts were too important to ignore. However, because they *were* unexpected there could be no fully objective means of measuring their incidence or meaning. Because I had proceeded purely along developmental lines I had applied no standard personality measures to the respondents. Therefore, I can only *infer* the impact of personality on modes of policy-thinking. Hence, it is possible that the bridging themes I will describe might not have impressed other readers of the interviews. I can only hope that my rendering is at

---

FOOTNOTE TO FIGURE 3:

*At a number of points in this essay one or another form of reasoning is characterized as "mature." This characterization is based upon the descriptions of the nine forms of policy reasoning outlined in this figure. Maturity is not meant as a value judgement, but rather refers to attainment of the skills outlined in the descriptions of each mode. In every case these descriptions are based on findings about the course of cognitive development derived from developmental psychology. Maturity involves successful attainment of these skills in the normal course of development. Maturity, therefore, refers only to the normal path of development along each mode, as verified by developmental studies of normal children and adolescents. "Maturity" refers therefore to a statistically verified concept of age-related change; not to some arbitrary "desirable" form of reasoning.

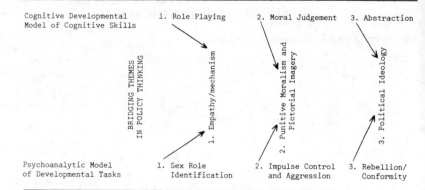

Figure 4: **BRIDGING THEMES IN ADOLESCENT POLITICAL THOUGHT**

least informed by a reasonable grasp of the personality, psychoanalytic, and cognitive development literatures.

Figure 4 links the developmental and psychoanalytic models of adolescence spelled out in Figures 1 and 2. The links between the two models express themselves via the three bridging themes which this essay describes and which the policy-reasoning interviews will be used to illustrate. As can be seen, the first bridging theme—empathy/mechanism—is the joint product of sex role identification and role-taking; the second—punitive moralism—is the joint product of impulse control and moral reasoning; and the third—political ideology—is the joint product of rebellion conformity and abstraction.

Let us now discuss and illustrate each of these bridging themes in detail. Before doing so, however, it is well to emphasize two things. First, these themes emerge clearly in but a minority of the cases examined. Only those adolescents who appear especially sensitive to a particular developmental task or to a particular cognitive skill manifest the appropriate bridging theme. We suspect, however, that such themes are at least latent in most adolescents. Second, these themes often manifest themselves *throughout* each interview and are not confined to the particular policy-reasoning measure—role-playing, moral judgement, and abstraction—through which they most commonly express themselves. Therefore, our examples will often be drawn from the interviews as a whole, rather than from the appropriate policy-reasoning mode.

II. THE EMERGENCE AND CRYSTALLIZATION OF ADOLESCENT BRIDGING THEMES

Bridging Theme I: Empathy/Mechanism

Students of human development have observed that emerging adolescent sex differences have much to do with variations in sensitivity to aggression. The literature demonstrates that males become preoccupied with aggression in adolescence, a preoccupation which some trace to the cultural norm of male independence (Alexander, 1969: 240). We see hints of these sex differences already expressing themselves among our seventh graders. Although talk of aggression colors many of our interviews, it predominates among boys. Aggressive images evidently constitute a powerful projection of male fantasy material.

In most cases respondents feared the presumed aggressiveness of others. Consider, for example, N., a seventh grade girl. I asked N. about the effects that prison disturbances might have on the rest of society, and she replied:

Well, maybe they might think it's cruel to bomb and stuff so that's probably the reason they do it. They probably think that this other guy didn't get, you know, he didn't get in prison because they didn't catch him, so they're going to try it.

Notice also the way N. reverses herself midway in answering a question about possible changes in the way prisons are operated. After having first argued that prisoners should be permitted more access to their relatives, she reconsiders:

Like their parents, but maybe their parents are robbers or something—they might just give them a gun or something to shoot down a guard or something. So maybe they shouldn't for that reason, and if they did, they should check the person, you know, when they come in to make sure they don't have a gun.

Fear of aggression also dominates N.'s answer to a hypothetical question about whether she would obey a newly lenient law toward prisoners that made her job as a prison guard more difficult:

Like, I would be scared of something—if a guy holds up a gun, what would you do?

Many young respondents link their aggressive fantasies to not entirely unreasonable beliefs that poor people or prisoners might seek revenge for ill treatment. Others, however, connect aggressiveness to a unique conception of human motivation. These latter respondents apparently assume that aggressive impulses can entirely circumvent the mind's strictures, thereby emerging spontaneously and uncontrollably. To such respondents the body is a machine which, once set in motion, cannot regulate itself. For example, B., a cryptic, relatively inarticulate seventh grade boy, argues that the reasons for prison violence are:

> (B) Maybe they [the prisoners] are just tired of getting pushed around.

> (Int) You think that a lot of people in prison they they are pushed around?

> (B) Maybe.

> (Int) Why do you feel that way?

> (B) Because they gotta do work there, and they tell them to hurry up and stuff like that.

B.'s response—indeed, his whole demeanor in the interview—has a flat, laconic, almost metallic quality that implicitly trivializes the reasoning capacities of prisoners. It exaggerates only slightly to say that B. views prisoners as automatons, directly controlled by outside stimuli, bereft of any internal censors. To B. and the others like him in the sample, many people are simply bundles of nerve ends housed in a Skinner box.

In contrast to the predominantly male preoccupation with aggression, seventh grade girls displayed a particular sensitivity to *feelings* and motivations as they touched on political problems. Other studies confirm that girls are encouraged early in their lives to focus upon affects and to react quickly to motivational nuances (Frank, 1951: 194). This sensitivity need not always lead to a particularly mature view of politics, however. Consider K., a rather slow, politically conservative girl. K.'s habit is to reduce every social problem to a matter of personal relationships and motivational states. For example, when she is asked initially to talk about the problems of prisons she remarks, "Well, some people might think that they don't deserve much or anything" and when asked to speak about the factors that cause prison tensions and riots she mentions "loneliness," and "no one comes to see them [the prisoners]." But K.'s sensitivity to motivational states eventually leads her into some rather bizarre byways. She believes that riots reflect only a personal conspiracy and she is particularly impressed by how easy it was to persuade people to riot in support of Angela Davis, implying that people are gullible when it comes to politics. Her sensitivity to motivation thus focuses her attention on a set of dramatic individual cases through which she reconstructs politics in miniaturized, manageable terms. In so doing, of course, she often ignores the complexity of the political process itself.

Like K., most seventh grade girls use their sensitivity to motivations and feelings as a supplement to the political traditionalism and conservatism that is modal for their age. This vision often seems founded on the felt necessity to appear respectable and likeable, as well as on the belief that social obstacles can be overcome by sheer personal commitment. S., a direct, rather quiet blond girl, exemplifies this tendency. When asked if poverty has any effects on the country, she immediately reduces the problem to a matter of individual appearances, expectations, and feelings.

> Well, I think that it does kinda have an effect, like if, like if you live in a good neighborhood, and the poor people, you know, like black people, so they move in and so it makes you look kinda poor too, and so I think it does have an effect.

Later in the interview I asked S. to decide whether she would favor an educational program for the poor preferred by an apathetic majority of poor people or a transportation program preferred by an intense minority of the poor. She resolved this dilemma by appealing to the notion of personal commitment:

> I think I would vote for to stay with the transportation, cause like if you don't really believe in . . . education strongly it might stop, you know, but transportation, if you believe in it, you know, it might . . . work better for you, you know, for the poor people.

As these two cases suggest, the female sensitivity to motivation, drives, and feelings usually serves a conventional—even occasionally biased—political outlook. Such an outlook, according to the developmentalists, is an important waystation on the road to political maturity. By contrast, the fear of aggression so commonly found among boys may well deter the progress of adolescent political reasoning, particularly in the area of role-taking (Jersild, 1963: 223). After all, role-taking requires the ability to see the point of view of others, and it is just this ability that fears of aggression undermine. We will provide more definitive evidence to support this contention shortly.

When we turn to our twelfth graders do we see any continuation of male concern with aggressiveness and female concern with empathy? And how do these motivational differences actually affect political role-taking?

At first glance the data seem disappointing. Mentions of aggressiveness and hostility are in fact rather infrequent among the older boys. However, a new theme emerges among twelfth grade males, one I believe to be a substitute for the earlier preoccupation with aggressiveness. A large number of the older boys, especially those who call themselves political independents, are notable for their extraordinarily detached and emotionally flat approach to social problems. [8] Above all, these boys are pragmatists, skeptical about human nature, and anxious to keep themselves clear of politically charged commitments. Let us examine two illustrative cases.

M., a twelfth grade boy, approaches political problems indirectly through economics. In answer to our first question about poverty, he remarks,

> I saw a movie in economics the other day that explained how the poor people actually paid more for the things they bought.

This remarks sets the tone for the rest of this interview, in which he concentrates on the economics of poverty. M.'s logical, analytical approach is certainly an advance over that of most seventh grade boys, of course, but it lacks the passion that could make him more than just a distant observer of social problems.

The roots of M.'s detachment reveal themselves in his response to a question which asked him to assess poverty's effects on the country. He remarks:

> Well, I think it probably more or less just affects the poor people. I don't think it has too much effect on me, unless you directly associate with it. If you're a social worker or someone in your family is poor themselves . . . America is sort of impersonal. Nobody really cares.

The impersonality which M. notes perhaps supplies a premise for his detached analytical reasoning style, but it does not in itself reveal the psychological motivation involved. The latter comes through in answer to another question, when M. remarks:

> If the poor people aren't held responsibile for their decisions or their actions why should anyone be held responsible? And society is just going to run wild, crime, and everything else and people are just going to do what they want to.

In M.'s case the fears of aggression so commonly found among early adolescent boys have found their antidote in an emotionally constricted, mechanical style of political reasoning. [9]

Self-protection has its costs, however, for M. can defend himself against his fear of agression only by mistrusting *any* form of emotional commitment or personal expression in politics. Elsewhere we asked him who should decide what should be done about prison reform, and he replies:

Well, I don't think it could be a group that was directly associated with it, because if you get really involved with anything then you think it's important, you know, personally. I think it should probably be the community as a whole. What they're interested enough to get involved with they should.

Thus, M. uses economics as a convenient method for lancing the emotional boil of politics. Other boys like him turn to technology or even social science for similar purposes. For example, B., also a twelfth grade boy, believes that "sociologists" should have the final decision about the importance of poverty, because they do not "exaggerate the truth." When asked initially to talk about poverty he offers what he himself calls a "technical definition"—"when a family makes a certain amount which makes them go on welfare." In the prison interview he turns from sociology to fashionable psychological jargon. "Psychologists study how prisons dehumanize people." And why should we do something about prisons? "We should so the crime rate would go down," not so that the prisoners themselves might get a fairer or more humane deal.

Of course, attention to expert advice, statistical rates, and economic processes mark a distinct advance over early adolescent political reasoning. Yet the reserve and detachment we detect among these boys hardly bespeaks a willingness to empathize and role play in politics. Where, then, does this male style originate?

My guess is that many adolescent boys can cope with their feelings of aggression only by projecting them outward onto the world-at-large and, later, by adopting a technologically sound, emotionally detached form of political thought as remedy. Calm reason thus provides intellectual armament against both the threatening world within and without. Technology apparently functions as a kind of political exorcism.[10] However, why boys should find the world threatening or feel particularly aggressive in the first place also deserves discussion. We shall examine the matter shortly.

Let it be understood, however, that mechanical reasoning is not the dominant style among twelfth graders. About half the boys and most of the girls display a fine balance between logical analysis and empathizing. J., a particularly personable girl, provides a good illustration. Asked what she would tell a child about prison problems and tensions, she, too, like B., uses the "dehumanization" jargon. However, notice the unusual context in which she embeds the term:

O.K., I think that most little children know what a jail is. They play jail and they say that's the bars and they know what it is and I'd use the word *dehumanization* and I'd explain it.

In order to test out what would be appropriate and necessary to say, J. casts herself in the role of a child. She plays roles spontaneously, not only here but elsewhere as well.[11] She remarks later in the interview:

> I think it's the conditions that the prisoners live in that make them riot. . . . I mean to live in a little hole like that it would drive me crazy, because I couldn't live like that and I think a lot of them get to the point where—twenty more years of my life—and they just rebel, I mean I think anyone would revolt.

To sum up, our guess is that sex role expectations in American society force males not only to establish an independent identity early in life, but also to impose that identity on a harshly competitive, aggressive, and impersonal world. Some boys react to these pressures by adopting a reasoning style that places sole reliance on their powers of detached analysis and pragmatic action. Girls escape these expectations, only to embrace their opposites. Girls are socialized early into a concern with emotional well-being and problems of motivation, no doubt in preparation for their nurturant roles as wives and mothers.[12] By late adolescence these pressures have made girls experts at spontaneously taking the roles of others. Sometimes, in fact, they let their empathy screen out logical considerations. Between these extremes, fortunately, we find a large group of emotionally sensitive and cognitively mature political thinkers drawn from both sexes.

The quantitative data on the role-playing mode of policy-reasoning support these conclusions. Girls scored considerably higher than boys on the role-playing mode.[13] Not only were girls better able to invent arguments opposed to their own views on poverty and prison reform, but they also were more likely to use moral and social welfare arguments rather than just pragmatic or instrumental arguments. Thus, empathy/mechanism bridges the gap between sex role development and role-playing quite well.

Bridging Theme II: Pictorial Imagery and Punitive Moralism

Impulse control constitutes a second major personality task in adolescence. The reemergence of Oedipal strivings gives rise to strong, hostile, possessive drives which must be controlled. Although it is impossible to be certain, one apparent method of discharging such impulses in early adolescence is through the medium of pictorial imagery. The coming of puberty infuses drama and action into the young adolescent's world. Life takes on a new visual aura, and this aura creeps into all aspect of political reasoning.[14]

Vivid pictorial imagery manifested itself continually throughout our seventh grade interviews. In some cases such imagery actually dominated the entire interview, particularly where, as at the outset of each interview, there was room for the respondent to describe in the most general, unfocused terms the problems he or she associated with poverty or prisons. Consider the following response by S., a seventh grade girl, to the poverty query:

> Well, poverty is when they don't have enough to buy food and their stomachs get bloated so they are really fat, and you see kids on T.V. and they don't look healthy at all and their ribs are sticking and they are really fat cause there is nothing in them.

S.'s response to the same question about prisons is similar:

> Well, it's not, they don't have very many things that they can do, like if they'd have better qualities in the prisons and more things that they could put in, you know, I mean I've seen a prison before and it is like, ah, they must have bunks and if they could just sorta fix it up and put things in that would make it . . . yeah, I know people do things wrong, but you know they could try to help them cause they would get out and they would tell everybody about how awful it is to be in prison, and they would say it is really bad; they don't have any nice things in there and the people that are in there, the police are trying to keep you quiet and everything, and, ah, they just shove you around, and they don't give you any first chance or anything, you do something and this is it.

Most of S.'s two interviews read like these examples. Successions of striking and evocative visual images, many of which contain explicit and implicit images of violence, tumble headlong upon one another. These are interspersed with offhand judgements, attributions of motives, and logical contradictions. As she encounters puberty S. finds her mind a sensitive screen upon which the projector of life haphazardly flashes one image after another. Her vivid imagination then elaborates and elongates this visual material even more colorfully.

Although S. is extreme in the *frequency* of her resort to imagery she is not at all atypical of the general *proneness* to imagery among seventh graders. Of course, these tendencies can take many different forms. Some respondents, for example, describe hypothetical vignettes in which they themselves play a central, occasionally heroic role. Consider B., a well-informed seventh grade boy with a taste for detailed interpretations, who responds to the query, "How do you decide when a law should be broken?" (in reference to a punitive law against the poor), by imagining the following scene:

> To break the law they passed, go to whoever, like the Governor or something who signed it, and ask him why. Just go, "Why can't we help the poor people? Why are they so different?" If you leave them alone they are going to be nothing but outcasts and people who are in poverty, that are going to cause more people to go in jail because they have to steal to live and when they steal, if they are caught, they have to go to jail.

It is difficult to attribute any long-term significance to the eruption of visual imagery in early adolescent political reasoning. We can, however, discern two contrary tendencies, one positive, the other negative.

The early adolescent's disposition to picture social problems in sensuous detail often seems an aid to political cognition. Visual imagery can convey an immediacy to political events that abstract understanding alone cannot provide. In such cases the pictorial sense becomes an invaluable catalyst for the development of political reasoning in adolescence. Indeed, our imaginative pictorial thinkers were disproportionately represented among our highest scoring respondents on most of the policy-thinking modes.

But a minority of respondents find their inflamed pictorial sense a mixed blessing. Youngers like S., in fact, seem almost to become fixated on visual imagery, apparently unable to employ other types of political cognition. It is impossible to be certain, but one can well doubt whether such youngsters will ever develop the detachment necessary to the maturation of abstract political reasoning. Perhaps it is the case that a little visual imagery goes a long way.

Our conclusions about punitive moralism can be slightly firmer, partly because from the outset of their investigations students of cognitive development have been preoccupied with the subject of moral reasoning (Kay, 1968), and partly because punitive moralism lasts into late adolescence, as pictorial imagery does not. Developmentalists have shown that the normal child slowly moves away from a punitive morality towards a morality of reciprocity and restitution, in which punishment becomes simply one limited instrument in the service of individual rehabilitation rather than an end in itself (Kay, 1968). But most developmentalists have not properly estimated the extent to which problems of impulse control make normal progress difficult and, in some cases, impossible. Where impulse control is a particularly serious problem for the individual, punitive moralism may be the result.

Punitive moralism was particularly noticeable in our prison reform interviews. In these interviews a punitive moralist was defined by the special stress placed upon the necessity for punishing prison inmates, by the belief that all those in prisons are automatically guilty of a crime, and by the conviction that law and order can only be founded upon a system of punishment. Punitive moralism is common among seventh graders, as the developmentalist paradigm would lead us to expect. What is unexpected, however, is the evident intrusion of ego-defences of various sorts into punitive moralism. Significantly, most such defences seemed to involve problems of impulse control. Such instances can only lead us to wonder whether personality formations solidifying in adolescence might not seriously inhibit development away from punitive moralism towards the morality of conscience and reciprocity. Let us examine some illustrative cases.

First, take J., a brittle, quick seventh grade girl, whose political views are relatively conservative for this particular sample and who identifies herself as a Republican. J. quickly establishes herself as especially concerned about the guilt of those in prison. She observes in answer to our initial general query:

(Int) What would you tell someone who knew nothing about prisons about the problems in prisons?

(J) Well, the things that they think is unfair to them. They don't think they get enough privileges but they did something wrong, you know. They need punishing in some way so they are put into prison and if they keep them on the streets they will just do it more and more. . . . Maybe teach them.

The origins of J.'s punitive moralism are difficult to discern, but there is one major clue that runs throughout her interviews. J. seems unusually anxious to present herself as a knowledgeable, worldly-wise girl, sophisticated beyond her years. Unfortunately for the reader, she conveys this image as much by visual style and manner as by rhetorical substance. Nevertheless, she answers questions in an unusually straightforward, almost blunt, and occasionally even callous fashion. Most evocative of this "tough," cynical style was her answer to the introductory question on the poverty interview:

That they didn't have much money and they weren't skilled in jobs and so they couldn't make much money and they just had to, you know, hang around in gangs and they get in fights and they hustle.

Of all our seventh graders J. was the only one to mention hustling, a practice which, as it turned out, she had learned about in one of her social studies classes. Her classmates had been exposed to the notion of hustling too, but J. alone used the concept spontaneously. Certainly her sensitivity to hustling allows her to establish her credentials as a realist—even a cynic—very rapidly indeed.

But more importantly, J's catalog of the vices of others permits her to project her own impulses outward. A punitive orientation is a natural consequence of such a projection, deliciously appealing to one who so readily sees baseness in her fellow humans. Why J. should need to see herself as tough, knowledgeable, and coolly in control we cannot say, of course, but we can at least guess that the persistence of such a self-image might decisively affect the maturation of her political morality.

A second example of punitive moralism provides an interesting contrast to J. L., another seventh grade girl, also spontaneously connects prisons to guilt and punishment. In answer to our initial query she observes:

> Oh, I'd probably tell them that a prison was a place where people did something wrong.

Later, in answer to our question inquiring about the causes of prison tensions and riots, she comments:

> Well, when they didn't have all those riots, they were really strict and nowadays they are not really very strict anymore and most people, most prisoners can really get away with anything except they might get caught at something they are not supposed to do.

Yet, throughout both interviews, L. presents a very different self from J. L. seems shy, almost meek in fact, and very anxious to please. Never is she as harsh as J. in her judgement of human nature. Indeed, on a scale of domestic liberalism we applied she scored high. The scale included questions about blacks and other deprived groups. Why, therefore, is she a punitive moralist?

The obvious answer to this question is her father, who is a policeman and, according to her unsolicited testimony, well-beloved indeed by his daughter. Perhaps what we hear from L. is just a father's warnings about prisons and criminals. But there are also other sources for her feelings; there are, in fact, fears and impulses she has yet to surmount. She admits:

> Sometimes I get scared at night and when I was little I usually got scared because on the T.V., like on the "F.B.I.", there usually is something at the end, you know, where they have "Wanted" and then they have this guy, how dangerous he was, and where he was found and so we would, I'd always run to the door and lock it and make sure—well, I was scared then but I'm not really now because I think I could handle the situation.

Thus, both timidity and toughness may serve to manage aggressive and fearful impulses, albeit at the cost of producing punitive moralism. Where it has put down so deep a set of psychological roots it is entirely possible that punitive moralism could distort the development of political evaluation hopelessly, fixating it at a primitive law and order level.

A particularly good example of the link between poor impulse controls and punitive moralism in *late* adolescence is provided by C., a twelfth grade boy. Both of C.'s interviews are dotted with passionate denunciations and rambling diatribes. Blacks and Indians could get ahead, but "they just don't want to change their attitudes:"

> My dad just got hired out not where we were working this summer, cause they had something else they had to do, but he said he doesn't think I can get a job unless in the office, cause I'm not black or any of the others.

Contemptuously, blacks are "lazy . . . lazy in the sense that they don't want to work or don't know how to work. Like give them a hero, like the Black Panthers or something, a hero so that they could see that if they work they could get up." He would choose better education over improved transportation for the poor, no matter what the poor themselves wanted, because:

> that's what I thought was better. I don't think they are stupid, but cause they were in the situation they are in they might not see ahead clearly. If they were capable of thinking ahead rationally, why are they so poor?

C. certainly does not shrink from stigmatizing and deriding his less fortunate fellow men. Curiously, however, he hesitates to evaluate his own conduct: "I'd break a law if I wasn't gonna get caught, I don't have any qualms about breaking a law." He is asked why, but all he can say is "I don't know." Elsewhere he observes, "I don't feel that bad breaking a law cause it's a law. But if I got spit on the sidewalk I'll have a guilty conscience. What's that, a hundred bucks?" (referring to the supposed fine for spitting on the sidewalk). Thus, where others are concerned C. is a punitive moralist, but where his own conduct is concerned, C. follows where impulse and interest lead. And sometimes his impulses lead to a rather nasty anger which sweeps away some crucial distinctions. What causes tensions and riots in prisons?

> (C) I don't know, just getting mad. Just getting fed up with those little psychologies . . . Problems. You just finally get mad enough.

> (Int) What causes people to get as dissatisfied in prisons as they have?

(C) I don't know. I don't know if they've ever been happy. I don't know if there's that much difference between being mad and killing somebody. It just flares up, maybe the temperature rises or something.

Is there any connection between C.'s anomie and his punitive moralism? Lane (1962) has speculated that people with poor impulse controls often project their assumptions about themselves outwards onto minorities, thus arriving at the conclusion that the deprived are irretrievably corrupt (Lane, 1962: chap. 3). Projection performs two functions in such a case. First, it substitutes an external moral compass for a defective internal compass. Second, it permits the continued free play of personal whim. Weak personal controls can thus turn morality from a standard of personal conduct into an instrument of political destruction. As these three cases illustrate, punitive moralism apparently stems either from the unfettered play of impulse or from its opposite, the repression of impulse. Punitive moralism thus bridges the gap between impulse control and moral judgement in politics.

Bridging Theme III: Ideology

Our interviews did not deliberately inquire into the home lives of our respondents or into their relationships with their parents. A small number of seventh graders nevertheless volunteered information about home and family; several mentioned having discussed political problems at home, while others told about their changing emotional relations with their parents. This vocal minority of students differed from their fellows in several interesting ways. Most important, they evidenced both a well-developed capacity for abstract reasoning and the beginnings of ideological thinking in politics. Therefore, it seems reasonable to think of ideology as a means of bridging the gap between the family tensions of adolescence and developing capacities to abstract. More specifically, political ideology can be a means of coping with the task of choosing a social identity, whether as rebel or as conformist.

Of course, students of political socialization have long been aware of the tie between parental political engagement and the emergence of secure political motives and reasoning in children (Prewitt, 1970: 58-83). But this is only a part of the total picture, for we find traces of ideology not only in children whose parents are overtly political but also in those whose parents are not. What then is the role of parents in the development of political ideology.[15] Let us examine four cases.

First consider R., a seventh grade boy. R. displays advanced conceptual, abstractive, and imaginative skills throughout both his interviews. Moreover, he is unusually political for his age. He demonstrates an exceptional awareness of the relationship between the public and its elected officials; he also displays an extraordinary ability to grasp the long-term consequences of political problems and public policies. These achievements are accompanied by a vivid pictorial imagination and are firmly undergirded by the conventional political morality typical of his age. In sum, given his youth, R. possesses an unusually well-balanced and cohesive set of political views. He seems, in fact, a nascent ideologue.

But equally striking is R.'s introduction of family themes into his conversations. For example, in reply to a question that asked him what he would do if a poverty program that he thought was fair to the poor was not working successfully, he observes:

> These people, they will probably think that everybody doesn't think of them, you know, like a lot of people like to be loved or something by their parents.

He returns to this rather wistful theme later in the interview, alleging that many poverty problems originate in disturbed relations between parents and children. At first, these remarks led us to the natural conclusion that he was projecting his own family difficulties outward. I doubt that this is so, however, for elsewhere, in commenting on a Kohlberg moral dilemma involving a boy's obligation to his parents, he states, "Maybe Joe [the hypothetical child in the dilemma] is like a lot of kids . . . like a lot of kids think more of their father than they do of themselves." R., in fact, is one of the few seventh graders who chooses to obey the father in this dilemma, rather than recommending disobedience on the part of the son. R. apparently respects his father, although he may doubt whether that respect is reciprocated in full measure. My own guess is that R.'s prescient sensitivity to family life and its problems provides him with a unique way of approaching politics. So fortified and stimulated, he finds it both necessary and congenial to develop the rudiments of a consistent, cognitively mature, affectively aware political position.

B., another seventh grade boy, provides a slightly more straightforward illustration of the family theme. B.'s interviews are heavily laden with information about politics and the social world, most of which he has harvested from the media. He displays an exceptional grasp of class structure for his age and shows a good feel for the intricacies of social problems.[16] Family concerns also manifest themselves throughout his two interviews. For example, he is unusually aware of the way marital disintegration and divorce cause problems in the ghetto. Is he projecting his own concerns? We cannot say with certainty, but again we have reason to be dubious, for at one point he observes:

> Sometimes when we are eating supper the issue of prison riots comes up at our table and we discuss it in our family. My father thinks it's wrong and my brother goes along with it and I think about it, though. I think sometimes it bothers me, cause it—you kind of like stay out of trouble because—they always tell me to watch out because if you do this, you don't go to jail, but your parents will.

B.'s fears of harming the parents for whom he apparently cares very much have tied him peculiarly closely to the political arena. More generally, B.'s political and cognitive maturation have been aided by a strong cathexis to his family and by his consequent sensitivity to family themes as they enter politics. For most seventh graders maturity is not contingent upon politicization, but for B. and R. it is. Their families have made politics a personally important problem that they must solve as part of their adolescence. To do so they are forced to think self-consciously about politics, and, in so doing, to take the first steps toward ideology.

As might be expected there was far more talk of family among our twelfth graders than among our seventh graders. This should not be surprising, for by twelfth grade the choice between rebellion and conformity is undoubtedly clearer than it is in seventh grade. Moreover, the urgency of making a choice between these alternatives is also greater in late than in early adolescence. Again we find that those who worked family themes into their interviews are comparatively advanced in their political thought as well as in their abstractive capacities.

S., a twelfth grade boy, provides a good example. S. is a strongly committed liberal. He demonstrates well-developed moral concern, sharp awareness of the class structure, empathy, spontaneous role-taking, and finally, comprehension of the full range of governmental activities. At one point he quite consciously recommends his own commitment to the poor as a kind of categorical imperative for political action. He calls his approach "humanist" and speaks of "my philosophy of human behavior."

> It's the humanistic approach more or less. Each man is born with an inherent potential. . . . The final goal would be self-actualization.

How much of this rhetoric is show and how much substance is difficult to say; yet, so far as we can tell, S. does possess a cohesive set of political ideas erected on a firm moral and cognitive foundation. Indeed, in one place he even directs us to Genesis for the source of his ideas.

From what family context do S.'s views derive? He tells us, "we've talked about it [poverty]. My dad donates money." Elsewhere he notes,

> The present problems there have been in prisons have been brought to the attention of me and my family, things that have been going

wrong. Maybe I have a unique family, but we discuss things like that.

S. seems proud of his family and his politics; to him becoming an ideologue is an accepted family role.

Few of our respondents were as sure of themselves politically or personally as S.; many, however, mentioned their families. In a number of these latter cases there clearly existed latent or manifest conflict between parents and child. For some the conflict had become so severe and general that it had spilled over into politics, thereby infusing the political realm with special significance for the child. Under these conditions we often saw our respondents self-consciously *working* at their politics, almost as if they believed that their lives depended on their solving the problem that politics symbolized. Perhaps they have become so exercised because they believe that a developed political stance can help liberate them from their parents. F., a plump, friendly girl, epitomizes this syndrome.

F.'s political views are generally middle-of-the-road, though she calls herself a Democrat. In any case, she is certainly not ideologically committed yet. She is also strikingly preoccupied by the necessity to appear respectable and "nice" to others, and she wishes that society too were composed of "nicer" people. At the same time, she distrusts—even despises—these rather conventional tendencies in herself:

> Right now, I'm at the age where my parents say I want you to believe in this God and go to this church, and I want you to do this, and wear these clothes, and meet my friends, and you grow up and you're kind of little and you love your parents, and you just teach your children and that's wrong. I think each person's born and comes into this world as an individual and as soon as they reach the age where they can reason and think and can do things for themselves, then they should become independent of their parents and perform their own idea and own law and society has no right to say what you think is wrong.

F. remarks elsewhere that she and her father argue about blacks and about where the responsibility for poverty lies. What she seems really to be saying is that her views—and her self—are in flux. Her conventionality is now a problem for her, even a vexation, certainly an increasingly hated sign of dependence on her parents. She reacts by empathizing rather broadly with the deprived; she says at one point she plans to join the Peace Corps.[17] Propelled by her need to use politics as a tool in the family power struggle, F. seems on the way to a sort of liberal-service ideology and to mature political reasoning. Thus, ideology may emerge either as a confirmation of family continuity and conformity—as in the case of S.—or as a badge of family disintegration and rebellion—as in the case of F.[18] But almost always it is those who are especially sensitive to family who make the leap to ideology.

III. SOME SPECULATIONS IN CONCLUSION

The main purpose of this essay has been to suggest the inadequacy of current single model theories of political socialization. Certain common forms of adolescent political reasoning, I have argued, cannot be understood except as by-products of the juncture between cognitive development and emotional development. Accordingly, I have called these forms of reasoning—empathy/mechanism, punitive moralism, pictorial imagery and, finally, political ideology—"bridging themes." Hopefully, these themes, which unite the cognitive developmental model of socialization to the psychoanalytic approach, point the way toward an integrated theory of political socialization.

Several qualifications regarding these themes are in order. It is important to remember that I applied no uniform measures of personality to the respondents. I *was* able to assess maturation in political *reasoning* more or less reliably with the aid of the policy-thinking scheme, but I possessed no analogous measures of personality tendency. Therefore, I could only infer an individual's position with regard to the three developmental tasks of impulse control, sex role identification, and rebellion/ conformity. This deficiency undoubtedly introduces a certain arbitrary quality into the analysis; I can only hope that the examples drawn from the interviews carry some conviction. Yet I would not deny that other investigators may have good cause for quarreling with certain of my interpretations.

Moreover, the three bridging themes themselves emerged clearly in but a minority of our respondents. This fact could be taken as evidence that, for most people, political reasoning eventually emerges unscathed by personality conflicts. Such a view would, of course, support the orthodox theoretical tack taken by the developmentalists. I could not subscribe to such a conclusion myself, however. After all, even the relatively straightforward majority displayed considerable variation in political reasoning, a fact difficult to explain without reintroducing some of the personality considerations we have been discussing. That bridging themes were not more numerous nor more widely distributed simply indicates that our instrument was defective in this regard, not that bridging themes are absent in most adolescents. Again, it is important to recall that from the outset the study was predicated mainly upon cognitive developmental lines.

Finally, let me hasten to say that I propose no sharp delineation between an "irrational" minority that suffers from severe personality disorders in adolescence and a "healthy," "rational" majority free of such disorders. Quite the opposite, in fact. Bridging themes are the natural outgrowths of junctions between cognitive and emotive development; they are not developmental aberrations. In any case, I have neither the training nor the inclination to describe one or another thought process as "pathological."[19] Nor, as I have stressed, did I apply research techniques that would have supported me in any such description.

Of course, I am not in a position to know whether the bridging themes I have described will extend beyond adolescence and become permanent additions to the intellectual equipment our respondents will bring to politics as adults.[20] Bridging themes may disappear with age, though I have hazarded some reasons for thinking this unlikely. Still, I cannot pretend to be in strong predictive position on the matter. The present essay, after all, should be viewed mainly as a preliminary effort in theorizing, identifying, and describing—not an effort in hypothesis testing.

We can now offer some specific hypotheses about the effects of bridging themes on adolescent political reasoning, however. These hypotheses might well guide a more rigorous investigation than that represented by my own endeavor. The present effort suggests the following hypotheses:

(1) *The young adolescent male's sensitivity to aggression* and hostility prevents the emergence of advanced role-playing and motivational awareness in political judgement.

(2) *The young adolescent girl's sensitivity to motivation* makes for a reasoning style sympathetic to political role-playing and empathy, although possibly lacking in abstract or formal qualities. However, motivational awareness is, on balance, a stimulant rather than a hindrance to political reasoning among girls.

(3) *Extreme reliance on pictorial imagery* in early adolescence retards the development of moral judgement in politics.

(4) *The punitive moralism and pictorial imagery* of many adolescents stems from problems of impulse control and projections of impulses onto the outside world, thus leading to a feeling of vulnerability in the face of a hostile, chaotic world. These tendencies may prevent the emergence of an internalized political conscience in late adolescence.

(5) *Young adolescents who are particularly attached to their families* and/or particularly aware of their parents' interest in politics are especially likely to develop a settled political ideology early in life.

(6) *Older adolescents whose relationships with their parents* depend heavily upon their own political development are very likely to become engaged political ideologues. These young people are of

two sorts: (1) those who see themselves following comfortably in a family political pattern, and (2) those who find themselves using politics as a means of settling a score with their parents.

Of course, whether these hypotheses deserve further investigation depends partly upon the value the prospective investigator places upon bridging themes. The arguments against further investigation seem formidable. A critic might well argue that bridging themes might at best account for some individual variations in a large sample of cases. But there has been no demonstration that bridging themes disturb more than slightly the main developmental trends of policy reasoning, nor that they distort such critical socialization processes as the transmission of partisan identification or the development of attitudes toward authority. Moreover, these latter processes yield easily to a single model treatment—either cognitive developmental or psychoanalytic. In addition, partisanship and attitudes toward authority may have a direct impact on the political system, whereas we can expect no comparable impacts from bridging themes.[21] Finally, any effort to uncover bridging themes on a large scale would necessitate costly, time-consuming depth interviewing, as opposed to easily interpretable, inexpensive survey research. In short, perhaps it is simply not worthwhile to investigate bridging themes any further.

One of these arguments can be dismissed quickly. The plain fact of the matter is that our use of survey research to link political orientations in childhood to subsequent political behavior and system response has generally failed (Searing et al., 1973: 415-433). Therefore, the fact that the bridging themes I have described will not yield readily to survey techniques is hardly cause for dismay; survey techniques have yet to prove their superiority over depth interviewing as a means of understanding the role of political socialization in the political system.

I would agree, however, that bridging themes probably do not impress themselves directly on the political system. Therefore, they can help us only inasmuch as they *refine* our understanding of political socialization. Many of the major socialization processes may not require such refinements; likewise, many may not demand interpretation via a complicated mixture of cognitive and psychoanalytic approaches to socialization.

Yet we should at least be clear about the fact that all socialization variables appear in the first instance as individual characteristics. Partisanship, attitudes toward authority, and political efficacy can be *measured* by survey research, but these measurements reveal only the surface manifestations of complex socialization processes which combine cognition and emotion. These factors can be treated within single models of socialization only by keeping the level of measurement deliberately gross and superficial. Deeper investigation of all these variables would no doubt reveal bridging themes akin to those discussed in this essay.

Therefore, to ignore bridging themes is to impose an artificially truncated socialization theory onto the data at hand, not to reflect the socialization process as it actually occurs. Generally speaking I have no quarrel with such an imposition; after all, most social science theories are, of necessity, artificial creations pitched at one or another level of abstraction (Winch, 1958). Moreover, I have no wish to commit the replicative fallacy commonly charged against phenomenological social science (Jarvie, 1972). My only point is that when there is no challenge to dominant social science practices we run the risk of blinding ourselves about our actual objects of investigation.

In sum, although single model accounts of socialization may be compatible with an artificial socialization theory, they bear little resemblance to the on-going process of socialization itself. By contrast, bridging themes combine theoretical interest with fidelity to the socialization process. They therefore reveal not only how dearly we pay for the artificial disjunction of one socialization theory from another, but also suggest new paths for socialization research to follow.

NOTES

1. The major breakthrough was the work of Joseph Adelson and his associates. For a summary of this work, with an excellent set of theoretical suggestions, see Adelson (1971: 1013-1050). For related research see O'Connor (1974: 53-79).

2. An excellent synthesis of cognitive developmentalism as it relates to socialization may be found in Kohlberg (1969: 347-480).

3. There are exceptions, however. Jennings and Niemi (1968: 443-467) concentrate on adolescence. A cognitive developmental approach to political learning in childhood is Devereux (1972: 99-125).

4. Indeed, longitudinal studies of human development undertaken by psychologists have rarely rested their findings on a well-developed theoretical base. For one notable example, see Block (1971).

5. I do not mean to imply that "tasks" do not vary with different generations of adolescents, nor that the tasks outlined might not permit alternative resolutions.

6. I refer here to the adult's well-known lack of either the ability or the inclination to apply abstract political principles to concrete cases. For a balanced consideration, see Erikson and Luttbeg (1973).

7. A test of coder reliability was undertaken to ascertain the utility of the coding scheme and of the nine modes themselves. Understandably, given the open-ended character of the interviews and the relative complexity of the scoring procedure, we expected anything but perfect agreement among our three judges. A subsample of 20 twelfth grade subjects was chosen for the test, utilizing Scott's formula, which computes agreement allowing for both number of scoring categories and distribution

of response within categories. Reliability coefficients so computed express the *"excess"* agreement over and above expected agreement, and is thus a conservative, stringent measure of reliability.

Reliability coefficients under this scheme were:

	Poverty Interview	Prison Interview
Abstract Reasoning	.085	.016
Causal Reasoning	.229	.071
Effect Reasoning	.249	.164
Moral Reasoning	.066	.168
Sociocentrism	.466	.656
Definitional Sociocentrism	.639	.383
Role Taking	.235	.278
Linkage	.348	.277
Hypothetical Thought	.365	.100

In virtually all cases coder agreement exceed that expected by chance. Moreover, it is important to remember that even in those cases where agreement did not exceed chance, the agreement that did exist was substantial and not necessarily *attributable* to chance. We expected that it would be harder for coders to agree on moral reasoning and abstract reasoning, since these modes of thought were qualitatively harder to assess, given our scheme, than for example the two forms of sociocentrism.

The data support the developmentalist assumption that each of these forms of thought develops with age. Twelfth graders scored higher on each form of thought than seventh graders. Moreover, the consistency of reasoning in each mode across policy areas was generally quite high, supporting developmentalist assumptions about the crystallization of modes of thought in adolescence. On Scott's measure of reliability, see Scott (1955: 321-325).

8. Perhaps these motivations underlie the slight propensity of Independents to be less interested in politics than other citizens. See, on this point, Flanigan (1972).

9. Perhaps this may even be seen as the forerunner of a slightly neurotic reasoning style. For amplification, see Shapiro (1964).

10. Donald Pike has suggested to me in conversation that the emphasis upon technology also has cultural determinants, and that, while technology may function as a means of political detachment in America, other cultures may provide different forms of political detachment for adolescents who feel a particular need to keep politics at bay.

11. Spontaneous role-playing probably depends upon the pre-existing mastery of the ability to interpret the behavior of individuals as involving intentions. This ability grows slowly in the early years. See Miller, et al. (1970: 613-623).

12. One wonders whether this process may not be changing under the impact of "women's liberation" movements and the more general secularization of female roles. If so, the results for political reasoning may be significant.

13. On the poverty interview the means were 2.242 for boys and 2.545 for girls. On the prison interviews the scores were 2.292 for boys and 2.844 for girls.

14. Many of our respondents were also indebted for the vividness of their imagination to television. On this point, see Baranowski (1971).

15. For a useful reconsideration of the entire range of parental influence on political socialization, see Connell (1972).

16. In general, one of the major differences between younger and older adolescents in our study was the explicit introduction of class analysis among the older students. Still, class analysis was hardly common; much less, indeed, than one might have expected from a reading of such works as Davies (1965).

17. Lane (1969) provides a very different interpretation of the origins of sympathy for the underdog.

18. Of course, the adoption of an ideology may itself be an independent contributor to *estrangement* from family, as well as the outgrowth of such estrangement. I am indebted to Donald Pike for this observation.

19. On the problems of deciding what is "pathological," see Smith (1972).

20. On this sort of problem see Marsh (1971).

21. For an argument that we ought only to look at socialization factors having a direct political impact, see Easton and Dennis (1969).

REFERENCES

ADELSON, J. (1971) "The political imagination of the young adolescent." Daedalus 100, 4 (Fall): 1013-1050.

――― and L. BEALL (1970) "Adolescent perspectives on law and government." Law and Society Rev. 4, 4 (May): 495-504.

――― and R. O'NEIL (1966) "Growth of political ideas in adolescence: the sense of community." J. of Personality and Social Psych. IV: 295-306.

ALEXANDER, T. (1969) Children and Adolescents: A Biocultural View. New York: Atherton.

BARANOWSKI, M. (1971) "Television and the adolescent." Adolescence 6, 1: 369-396.

BEST, J. J. (1973) Public Opinion. Homewood, Illinois: Dorsey.

BLOCK, J. (1971) Lives Through Time. Berkeley: Bancroft.

BLOS, P. (1962) On Adolescence: A Psychoanalytic Interpretation. New York: Free Press.

CONNELL, R. W. (1972) "Political socialization in the American family: the evidence re-examined." Public Opinion Q. 36, 2 (Fall): 323-333.

――― (1971) The Child's Construction of Politics. Melbourne: Melbourne Univ. Press.

DAVIES, A. F. (1965) "The child's discovery of social class." Australian and New Zealand J. of Sociology 1, 1: 21-38.

DAWSON, R. E. and K. PREWITT (1969) Political Socialization. Boston: Little, Brown.

DEVEREUX, E. C. (1972) "Authority and moral development in German and American children: a cross-national pilot experiment." J. of Comparative Family Studies 3, 1 (Spring): 99-125.

EASTON, J. and J. DENNIS (1969) Children in the Political System. New York: McGraw Hill.

ELKIND, D. (1969) "Egocentrism in adolescence," pp. 497-507 in R. Grinder [ed.] Studies in Adolescence, 2nd ed. New York: Macmillan.

ERIKSON, E. (1968) Identity, Youth and Crisis. New York: Norton.

ERIKSON, R. S. and N. R. LUTTBEG (1973) American Public Opinion: Its Origin, Content, and Impact. New York: Wiley.

FLANIGAN, W. H. (1972) Political Behavior of the American Electorate. Boston: Allyn & Bacon.

FLAVELL, J. H. (1968) The Development of Role-Taking and Communication Skills in Children. New York: Wiley.

FRANK. L. K. (1951) "Personality development in adolescent girls." Monographs of Society for Research in Child Development 16, Serial No. 53: 194.

GALLAGHER, J. R. and H. HARRIS (1958) Emotional Problems of Adolescents. New York: Oxford Univ. Press.

GREENSTEIN, F. I. (1968) "Political Socialization," pp. 551-555 in D. L. Sills [ed.] International Encyclopedia of the Social Sciences. New York: Macmillan and Free Press.

HAAN, N., M. SMITH, and J. BLOCK (1968) "Moral reasoning of young adults: Political-social behavior, family background, and personality correlates." J. of Personality and Social Psych. 10, 2 (November): 183-201.

HARMON, C. P. (1973) The Development of Moral and Political Reasoning Among 10, 13 and 16-Year-Olds. Unpubl. dissertation, Yale University.

HESS, R. D. and J. TORNEY (1967) The Development of Political Attitudes in Children. Chicago: Aldine.

INHELDER, B. and J. PIAGET (1958) The Growth of Logical Thinking From Childhood to Adolescence. New York: Basic Books.

JARVIE, I. C. (1972) Concepts and Society. London: Routledge & Kegan Paul.

JENNINGS, M. K. and R. NIEMI (1968) "Patterns of political learning." Harvard Educ. Rev. 38, 2: 443-467.

JERSILD, A. (1963) The Psychology of Adolescence, 2nd ed. New York: Macmillan.

JOSSELYN, I. M. (1971) Adolescence. New York: Harper & Row.

KAY, W. (1968) Moral Development. London: Allen & Unwin.

KOEPPEN, S. R. (1970) "Children and compliance: a comparative analysis of socialization studies." Law and Society Rev. 4, (May): 545-564.

KOHLBERG, L. (1969) "Stage and sequence: the cognitive development approach to socialization," pp. 347-480 in D. Goslin [ed.] Handbook of Socialization Theory and Research. Chicago: Rand McNally.

——— and C. GILLIGAN (1971) "The adolescent as a philosopher: the discovery of self in a postconventional world." Daedalus 100, 4 (Fall): 1051-1086.

LANE, R. E. (1969) Political Thinking and Consciousness. Chicago: Markham.

——— (1962) Political Ideology. New York: Free Press of Glencoe.

MARSH, D. (1971) "Political socialization: the implicit assumptions questioned." British J. of Polit. Sci. 1, 4 (October): 453-465.

MERELMAN, R. and A. McCABE (1974) Evolving orientations towards policy choice in adolescence." Amer. J. of Polit. Sci. (November).

MERELMAN, R. (1973) "The structure of policy-thinking in adolescence: a research note." Amer. Polit. Sci. Rev. 67 (March): 161-166.

——— (1971) "The development of policy-thinking in adolescence." Amer. Polit. Sci. Rev. 65 (December): 1033-1047.

——— (1969) "The development of political ideology: a framework for the analysis of political socialization." Amer. Polit. Sci. Rev. 63 (September): 750-767.

MILLER, P., F. KESSELL, and J. FLAVELL (1970) "Thinking about people thinking about people thinking about . . . a study of social cognitive development." Child Development 41, 3 (September): 613-623.

O'CONNOR, R. E. (1974) "Political activism and moral reasoning: political and apolitical students in Great Britain and France." British J. of Political Science 9, 1 (January): 53-79.

PEEL, E. A. (1971) The Nature of Adolescent Judgement. London: Staples.

PIAGET, J. (1965) The Moral Judgement of the Child. New York: Free Press of Glencoe.

PREWITT, K. (1970) The Recruitment of Political Leaders. Indianapolis: Bobbs-Merrill.

SCHONFELD, W. R. (1971) "The focus of political socialization research: an evaluation. World Politics 23, 3 (April) 544-578.

SCOTT, W. A. (1955) "Reliability of content analysis: the case of nominal scale coding." Public Opinion Q. 19 (Fall): 321-325.

SEARING, D. D., J. J. SCHWARTZ, and A. E. LIND (1973) "The structuring principle: political socialization and belief systems." Amer. Polit. Sci. Rev. 68, 2 (June): 415-433.

SHAPIRO, D. (1964) Neurotic Styles. New York: Basic Books.

SMITH, M. B. (1972) "Normality: for an abnormal age," pp. 102-130 in D. Offer and S. Freedman [eds.] Modern Psychiatry and Clinical Research: Essays in Honor of Roy E. Grinker, Sr. New York: Basic Books.

――― (1969) Social Psychology and Human Values. Chicago: Aldine.

―――, N. HAAN, and J. BLOCK (1970) "Social psychological aspects of student activism." Youth and Society 1, 2: 261-288.

WINCH, P. (1958) The Idea of a Social Science. London: Routledge & Kegan Paul.

WITKIN, H. (1962) Psychological Differentiation. New York: Wiley.

RICHARD M. MERELMAN is a Professor of Political Science at the University of Wisconsin, Madison. He Holds B.A. and M.A. degrees from George Washington University and the University of Illinois, and he earned his Ph.D. at Yale University. He is the author of Political Socialization and Educational Climates: A Study of Two School Districts (1971) and the forthcoming Flowering of Political Reasoning: Political Thought in Adolescence. His numerous articles have appeared in such publications as the American Political Science Review and Journal of Politics.